W9-ADS-842

Presented to

_____

with love from

_____

_____

Prayers for Girls

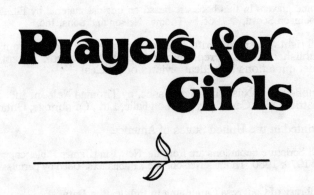

THOMAS NELSON PUBLISHERS
Nashville • Camden • New York

Fourteenth printing

Copyright © 1981 by Thomas Nelson, Inc., Publishers

Some prayers in this book are based on original material by Elizabeth Robinson Scovil, © 1966 by Thomas Nelson and Sons, Inc.

All rights reserved. Written permission must be secured from the publisher to use or reproduce any part of this book, except for brief quotations in critical reviews or articles.

Published in Nashville, Tennessee, by Thomas Nelson, Inc. and distributed in Canada by Lawson Falle, Ltd., Cambridge, Ontario.

Printed in the United States of America.

All Scripture quotations are from the New King James Bible, copyright © 1979, 1980, Thomas Nelson, Inc., Publishers. Used by permission.

Library of Congress Cataloging in Publication Data

Main entry under title:

Prayers for girls.

   Includes index.
   Summary: A collection of short prayers for all occasions, written especially for girls.
   1. Girls—Prayer-books and devotions—English.
[1. Prayers]
BV283.G5P7   1981   242'.82   81-14064
ISBN 0-8407-5242-3   AACR2

Contents

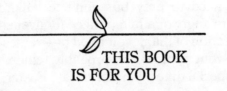

THIS BOOK
IS FOR YOU

Have you ever had a diary? Or do you have a very special friend—a boy or a girl or a dog or a cat—that you tell everything to?

God wants you to tell your most private thoughts and feelings to Him in prayer—even the ones you think no one else will understand. This book is for that very purpose: to show you how you can talk to God freely, but respectfully, as you would talk to a good Father.

This book is for you, to keep hidden away in your drawer, or to carry with you on trips, or to put under your pillow to read at night and in the morning. Sometimes, you may even want to let your parents or your grandmother or a special friend read it with you, too. It tells you about praying, and it is divided into six sections.

I Want to Be Like You, God is an important section, for you need constantly to ask God to make you act like Him: loving, gentle, patient, self-controlled. *When I Feel . . .* is especially for those times when you need to pray but don't feel like it—like when you're angry or afraid or need forgiveness. Part III is a collection of thank you prayers—verses for mealtimes that your parents will probably remember. Part IV is for special times: your birthday, Easter, when you are sick, or before your softball game.

God wants to hear about *your* desires in prayer, but He also wants you to pray for other people. That's what Section V is about. Part VI, *Some Famous Prayers*, gives examples of how you might want to pray someday, too. There are prayers of Saint Augustine, John Wesley, and even Saint Patrick.

There are blank pages at the end of the book where you can write your own prayers—maybe things you want to pray for every day, or a prayer you've heard that you want to remember. There's an index on page 125 to help you when you want to go back and find one special prayer in this book.

Jesus prayed to God His Father all the time, about everything that He saw or thought or felt—and He never felt embarrassed or silly about praying. Prayer was like breathing for Him, because He knew God always wanted to listen. We hope this book will help you pray that way, too.

The Editors

Prayers for Girls

THE LORD'S PRAYER

Our Father in heaven,
Hallowed be Your name.
Your kingdom come.
Your will be done
On earth as it is in heaven.
Give us this day our daily bread.
And forgive us our debts,
As we forgive our debtors.
And do not lead us into temptation,
But deliver us from the evil one.
For Yours is the kingdom and the
   power and the glory forever.
   Amen.

MATTHEW 6:9–13

PART I

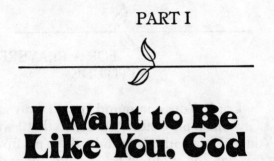

I Want to Be Like You, God

. . . the prayer of the upright is His delight.

PROVERBS 15:8

FOR A PRAYERFUL ATTITUDE

Lord, You command me to pray all the time.* Give me a prayerful attitude, so that I will talk with You as I talk with my friends. Keep me from just going through the motions and using empty words. When I do not know how to express myself, help me to be honest and sincere. Make me realize how I have neither been thankful nor sorry for my sins. Give me more love for Your Word and for Your companionship. I want to be a true disciple of You all my life. Help me today to wait before You in prayer. In Your name, amen.

---

*1 Thessalonians 5:17

TO LOVE GOD

God, You have loved me all my life. Fill my heart with such love for You that I will be able to do the things that are pleasing to You. You are always with me and know every little thing I do, guiding and guarding me from harm. May Your goodness make me depend on You. Help me to love and serve You while this life lasts, so I will know the fullness of Your love and the sweetness of being with You in person in heaven. In Jesus Christ's name, amen.

TO LOVE OTHERS

God, You teach me in Your Holy Word that all my good works are worth nothing without love.* Put into my heart Your love, so that I can love everyone. Help me show this love by my actions. Teach me to be loving when I watch other people. When they get into trouble, remind me how sinful I am. Show me how to help them instead of condemning them, remembering how easy it is to do wrong. Keep me from believing the worst about people. Make me quick to see when they want to do right. I want to help them by being sympathetic and a real friend. In Jesus' name, amen.

---

*1 Corinthians 13

TO BE
UNSELFISH

Lord Jesus, in Your life here You showed me the perfect example of love for others. Free me from thinking about myself all the time. You said that the one who loses life shall find it, so help me forget about putting *me* first. Teach me how a heart that loves others is happier than a heart that says, "Me first." Teach me how to find joy in helping others, and how to give without expecting something in return. Keep the thought of Your own unselfish life always before me. In Your dear name, amen.

TO TRUST
IN GOD

God, You are powerful enough to make this world and to put me in it. Help me to trust You. My problems are small, but they are a part of Your great plan and You care about them. Make me sense Your presence with me in my daily life, and make me know that nothing can separate me from You. You watch over the birds of the air, and You tell me in Your Word that I am more valuable than the sparrows. So give me, too, the things that I need. Help me not to worry. In Jesus' name, amen.

FOR FAITH

Lord, there are many things I cannot understand. But I know that in the next world all mysteries will be made clear to me. Make plain to me what I need to know. Help me to follow in the footsteps of Your holy life. I want my daily life to show that I have faith in You. Give me light to walk by. Thank You for Your Holy Spirit, who will lead me in truth. For Your own dear sake, amen.

TO BE FAITHFUL

Lord Jesus, You have given each of us chores to do on earth. Teach me to be faithful as I do mine. Help me to do each one as if You were physically here with me, so that I will do the best I can. If my work is boring or harder than I thought it would be, help me to keep on and not give up, just because I am tired of it.

Teach me also to be faithful to my friends. Help me never to tell a secret. Remind me not to reveal what I overheard by accident, nor to tell things I know my friends or parents wouldn't want told. Make me worthy of trust. For Your own sake, amen.

FOR PATIENCE

Lord Jesus Christ, in Your life on earth You showed the example of perfect patience. Help me to live through my problems without complaining. Make these trials that seem so hard bring good to me. Teach me how to keep all my strength for patient waiting, and not to waste it in tears or griping. Teach me how to wait.

Help me remember that all good is slow in growth, and keep me from despair because I don't see results at once. When I am aggravated with others, remind me of my own failings, and make me patient with their faults. In Your name, amen.

FOR HUMILITY

God, I know You hate the proud and give help to the humble. Make me humble. Help me to understand that the things I am proud of are gifts from You and are to be shared with others. When I am tempted to be proud and haughty, remind me that You did not give me good things because I deserved them. Teach me how to use them so they will be a blessing and not a curse to me. Lead me like a child and teach me how to trust in You. In Jesus' name, amen.

FOR
SELF-CONTROL

God, I ask You to order my mind so that I will have all my thoughts and desires under control. When temptation comes, make me ready to meet it. If fear comes over me, give me strength to conquer it. Keep me calm in danger and unruffled when panic seizes others. When I am annoyed, teach me how to talk things out kindly. If others provoke me, teach me how to settle things in love.

Give me power to control my emotions. Give me a calm that will make me able to think and work and play the best I can. Keep my trust in You unshaken. In Jesus' name, amen.

TO BE STRONG

God, You make strength perfect in weakness.* I am weak. I pray You will give me the strength I am missing. Give me as much as I need. When I want to sin, deliver me by giving me the power to win over temptation. When my daily work is too hard for me, strengthen me to be able to do it. Lighten the load as You see fit, so that my strength will be equal to it. You have made many others strong. Make me strong, too. In Jesus' name, amen.

---

*2 Corinthians 12:9

FOR
CHEERFULNESS

Lord, make me cheerful, so that I can make those around me glad. Remind me that the world is full of sadness and needs all the brightness I can give it. Help me give my griefs to You so that I will bring only happy thoughts to others. Help me to keep cheerfulness like a shining armor around me. When I am sad, help me not to forget that there is still joy on earth, and in a little while I will share in it again. I ask this in Jesus' name, amen.

TO BE FAIR

God, You are the Judge of all the earth. Give me the spirit of fairness. Get rid of all my mean thoughts, and make me able to see the rights of others. Keep me from being biased by the way I feel. It is so easy for me to jump to conclusions. Keep me from doing that. Help me treat others as I want them to treat me and teach me to be fair to myself. In Jesus' name, amen.

TO BE
GENEROUS

Lord, give me a generous heart, so that I am ready to give my best to others. Everything I have—time, talent, money—comes from You. I want to be willing to share it with those who need it. Make me quick to see when others do well, and to give them their just share of credit and praise.

Help me to be ready and generous with forgiveness, too. Help me to be generous to those I do not like or who seem to me not to deserve it. For Jesus Christ's sake, amen.

FOR TACT

Lord, You are full of love and mercy. Help me to be careful about other people's feelings. Keep me from saying something without thinking, or asking the wrong question—things that can hurt as badly as a slap in the face. Show me how to put shy people at ease and to give them confidence by being kind and really interested in them. Keep me from snooping into other people's private business. Help me to be thoughtful. Bless me with keen insight so that I will see at once the right thing to do or say—or when I should be quiet. In Jesus' name, amen.

TO SAY THE RIGHT THINGS

God, You gave me the wonderful gift of speech to share my thoughts with others. Help me to use it rightly. Teach me how to speak the truth in love, never with the wish to harm or embarrass someone else. If I know something bad about someone, help me to keep it to myself. Keep me from hateful words and from taking Your precious name in vain by using it to emphasize what I say. For Jesus' sake, amen.

FOR AN
OPEN MIND

Give me, Lord, I ask, an open mind, ready to receive the truth and ready to act upon it. Show me that others have the right to their own opinions, and help me to see their point of view. Make me ready to say that sometimes I might be wrong. Help me not to shut my mind to facts simply because I do not like them. Help me to see those facts as clearly as the facts that are on my side. Open the eyes of my soul to see the truth. In Jesus' name, amen.

FOR WISDOM

God, You know that it is hard for me sometimes to know what is right. Give me the wisdom I need to see how I can please You. Thank You for Your Holy Spirit, who guides me. Help me to do what is best in Your eyes and best for those who depend on me. Give me wisdom to discern between what is false and what is true, so I will not be tricked or fooled by what looks good or my own selfishness. I ask this in Jesus' name, amen.

TO KNOW WHAT
I AM LIKE

God, You know what people are like because You made us. Teach me to know myself. Show me my weaknesses, so that I can be strong to overcome them. Keep me from being filled with pride when I should be ashamed of my own foolishness. Give me confidence in myself when there is work to be done. Help me to look at why I really want things and not to make excuses for conduct I should condemn. Make me able to see when I am wrong and to admit it. In Jesus' name, amen.

FOR PURITY

Lord Jesus, You lived a perfect life on earth. Make me as pure and clean in soul and body as You are. When temptation is strong, help me remember that the pleasure of a moment is not worth the soil of sin. Guard my mind from impure thoughts or the beginnings of evil. Make me know that I will hate myself if I give way to sin. Teach me to honor my body as the temple of the Holy Spirit. In Your name, amen.

FOR MODESTY

Lord, You have set limits on speech and behavior to protect me. Help me keep in those boundaries. Give me moderation in everything I say and do. When I feel that something is immodest, help me to avoid it. Teach me how to dress so I will look decent and pleasing and modest, without making myself conspicuous. When fashion makes this hard, give me the courage to dress the way I know pleases You. Keep me from repeating dirty jokes or stories. Make me so that I won't take pleasure in anything that is evil. In Jesus' name, amen.

TO BE HEALTHY

All-powerful God, You have given me a wonderful body to hold my soul. Teach me how to live so I can stay healthy. Help me learn the laws that keep my body in good shape. Help me to regulate my appetite and my desires so that they will serve me. Give me a healthy mind, with clean and pure thoughts. Make me love Your good gifts of fresh air and cool water, so that I will use them for the good of my body. Keep me always fit to serve You. In Jesus' name, amen.

FOR A
SERVANT'S HEART

Lord Jesus, You came into the world not to be served, but to serve. Give me, I pray, the heart of a servant. Help me to see what I can do for the good of others. Show me how to help those who are near me—my family, my neighbors, and my classmates at school. Make me considerate of the weak, the elderly, and the unfortunate. Show me what I can do for them. If I can help out, make me glad to do it.

Teach me that a heart that looks for ways to do good to others has more happiness than the heart that does good only for *me*. By unselfish service, make me learn that it is better to give than to receive. In Jesus' name, amen.

TO OBEY
MY PARENTS

Lord Jesus, You were subject to Your parents. Give me, I pray, the same spirit, so that like You I will reverently love and obey my parents. I want to love them more and more each day and to show my love by my willing obedience to what they want. Help me to obey cheerfully. Help me to be helpful. Fill me with love, so that I will honor them. In Your name, amen.

THE RIGHT
KIND OF FRIENDS

God, help me to make the right kind of
friends. Your Holy Word warns that bad company will
ruin a good character.* Help me to learn how good it
is not to spend time with those who do wrong or who
can do nothing but make fun of other people.

Help me see that it is easier to make bad
friends than it is to get rid of them. People will think
that I am like the people I spend my time with. Help
me to avoid the wrong kinds of friends, and instead to
be a leader in doing good.

Keep me from hanging around with people
who are lazy, for Satan will find mischief for idle
hands to do. In Jesus' name, amen.

---

*Proverbs 13:20

TO LEARN
AT SCHOOL

God, You have made it a rule of life that learning is hard work. Give me an earnest heart to make the best use of my classes at school. Bless my teachers, and give me a heart to learn. Help me continue studying hard, even when I want to quit. By doing faithfully the things I know I should, may I grow to love my work. If school work is hard for me, help me to remember that You give a crown to those who keep trying. I want to follow Jesus, who always pleased You. In His name, amen.

PART II

When I Feel . . .

. . . For we do not know what we should pray for as we ought, but the Spirit Himself makes intercession for us. . . .

ROMANS 8:26

WHEN
I CAN'T PRAY

God, You see that I feel like I can't pray. Fill my heart with such love for You that I will come to You in trust, knowing that You are near to help me. I don't need lots of words, for You know my most secret thoughts. I bring all my troubles and disappointments, doubts and fears to You, because You are my Father. Chase away everything that makes me doubt You. Make me know that You are always ready to hear and help me, because You love me. In Jesus' name, amen.

WHEN
I'M ANGRY

Lord, You know how often I want to say angry words or to do something I will later be sorry for. I don't agree with someone, and it is hard for me not to think they are stupid or silly. Help me to stop and think, and not to start a fight. Keep me from saying things I know will make people mad. Teach me to be quiet and not let others tease me into ugly answers. When this seems impossible, remind me how You were with Your enemies, so that I can follow Your example. For Your glory, amen.

WHEN THERE'S
FIGHTING AT HOME

God, You can help people who live in a house together to get along. Bring peace into our home. Help me to do my share. Prepare me to be ready always to give the gentle answer that cools anger. Take away my desire to irritate others, and prevent me from saying the angry words that stir up quarrels. If I am tempted to fight, make me able to keep my own temper. When my feelings are hurt, teach me to turn to You for comfort. Keep me calm under the shadow of Your wing. In Jesus' name, amen.

WHEN I
MUST DECIDE

God, You have made me with the power to choose good or evil and have given me a free will to do so. Guide me to a right decision today. Give me an open mind, so that I can see both sides of the question and understand what is really important. Keep me from being deceived by appearances. Teach me how to look to the heart of things and to see what is beneath the surface. Prevent syrupy words and flattery from distracting my judgment and taunts and threats from disturbing it. Help me to decide according to what is right. In Jesus' name, amen.

WHEN I NEED
TO FORGIVE

Lord, You have taught us to ask for forgiveness from You. Make me able to forgive those who have hurt me. Soften my heart, so that I will not harm them. If bitter thoughts are in my mind and cruel words come to my lips, help me to be silent. Clean my heart of all anger and resentment. I can't make things right by revenge. Make me able, always, to forgive completely and from my heart. In Jesus Christ's name, amen.

WHEN I NEED
FORGIVENESS

God, You never hate Your children, no matter how badly we have sinned. Please forgive my great sin. I have fallen so low I hardly dare to come to You. You know how weak I am. Forgive me for giving in to wrong. If I were not Your child, I would not be sorry for what I have done. Give me true repentance and put behind me the sin I have committed. Let me show that I am sincerely sorry by never doing it again. If I have made others sin too, give me strength to try to help them do better. Thank You for Your patient love for me. In Jesus' name, amen.

WHEN I WANT
TO LIE

God, You have told me in Your Word that You are the truth.* Keep me from lying. Don't let fear force me into saying what is not true. Make me think before I speak, so that what I say will be accurate and true. Strengthen me when it is hard to tell the truth. Make me realize how important it is to keep my word. Help me promise only what I know I can do. Make me sincere in all my actions. Take away the wish to deceive, so that I will be truthful in both word and deed. I ask this in Jesus Christ's name, amen.

———
*John 14:6

WHEN I WANT
TO STEAL

God, I am tempted so badly to steal. Give me strength to resist. Give me such respect for the rights of others that I will not hurt them. Make me guard their belongings as I do my own. Make me honest with myself, so I will know myself for what I really am and not for what I pretend to be. Forgive me for coveting. Help me not to make it hard for others to be honest, by putting temptation in their way. I ask this in the name of Jesus Christ my Lord, amen.

WHEN I NEED MONEY

Lord, You know I need many things that money can buy. Teach me how to earn money honestly and to spend it wisely. You have given us so much in this world of Yours. Teach me now how to use your gift of money, so I will never be burdened by poverty or worry. If I have lots of money as I get older, help me to remember it comes from You. Teach me to use it for Your service and for the good of others. In Jesus' name, amen.

WHEN I DON'T
KNOW WHAT TO DO

God, I just don't know what to do. I can't see what is right and what is wrong. Send me light and guidance. Take my hand and lead me. Show me what You want me to do, and help me to do it. Guide me by Your Holy Spirit so that I won't make a mistake. I want to do what is right and best for me and those who are nearest to me. In Jesus' name, amen.

ON A GLOOMY DAY

God, my life is dark and full of sorrow. There seems to be nothing to look forward to but sadness. Show me that life still has duties and many pleasures in store for me. Revive in me the desire to live. Plant hope in my heart so that my despair will vanish, like the dew before the sun.

All good things come from You. You have promised to give them to those who love You. Fulfill Your promise to me. Give me hope in You to brighten my way here. In Jesus' name, amen.

WHEN I'M DEPRESSED

Dear Lord, my heart is weak and I have no strength left. Everything I do turns out wrong. It makes no difference to anybody what I do. Everybody seems to hate me. I know that You have a place in Your world for every child of Yours. Show me my place. No one else can take my spot, for in all this great universe there is nobody just like me. Comfort me by showing me how much You love and care for me. Make me sure I can be what You want me to be. In Jesus' name, amen.

WHEN I'M TIRED
OF BEING GOOD

God, You have given me the wish to do right. Now, strengthen me to keep on doing good. When I am tired of doing right, remind me that the way of sin is hard in the end. When I am discouraged, let me feel Your presence. Help me to continue as a good disciple of Jesus Christ. In Jesus' name, amen.

WHEN I WANT
TO COMPLAIN

God, You have put me where You want me in this world. Help me not to complain. Give me the ambition to improve things I don't like. Help me to be content when I can't change things, so I won't waste my strength and make others miserable by useless griping. Help me to realize that complaining changes nothing and interferes with fruitful action. Teach me to bring all my complaints to You first, and to pour out my heart to You. Then help me to listen to Your answer. In Jesus' name, amen.

WHEN I'M
WORRIED

Lord, my mind is tossed about like the waves of the sea and filled with doubt and trouble. Calm me and keep me calm in the middle of all these problems. I know that I am safe in Your protection. Open my eyes so that I can see Your loving care surrounding me. Make me feel secure. Help me to trust You as my tender Father. You have said, "In quietness and in confidence shall be your strength."* Help me put away the doubts and fears that are worrying me. You have promised to keep me in perfect peace if my mind is focused on You.* Fulfill that promise to me. In Jesus' name, amen.

*Isaiah 30:15; 26:3

WHEN I HAVE
FORGOTTEN ABOUT GOD

God, You are my heavenly Father; yet I have forgotten You. My days have been full of what I wanted to do, without a thought of what pleases You. Open my eyes to see how this hurts You, and change my heart so that I will want to spend time with You. Help me to think of You more constantly. Teach me to pray about everything. Help me to listen for Your voice within and always to obey You. I want to devote my life to You. In Jesus' name, amen.

WHEN I SEE
SOMEONE DO WRONG

Lord, You made me my brother's keeper, but help me not to irritate my family and friends if I see them doing wrong. Teach me to say something about it once, and not to keep up a constant nagging. Instead, make me think of pleasant words to help them change. Encouragement will do far more than criticism. Show me when to stop talking, so that I will not make others resent me. Prevent me from making myself feel better by scolding. Help me to talk to You about it. I ask this in the name of my patient Master, Jesus, amen.

WHEN I WANT
TO GOSSIP

Lord, You teach me in Your Word to love my neighbor as myself.* Keep me from hurting anyone by thoughtless words. Close my mouth, so I won't repeat stories that may not be true. Make it a rule of my life never to talk about others behind their back or to tattle. Let kindness control my tongue. Make me slow to jump to conclusions. Make me realize the words I say can never be taken back. Remind me always to think before I speak. I ask this in Your name, amen.

---

*Mark 12:31

WHEN I THINK
I'M BETTER THAN
ANYONE ELSE

God, You give every good and perfect gift.* Keep me from boasting about what You have given me. If I have beauty, let me rejoice in it. But help me to remember that it did not come to me because I deserved it or worked for it. You gave it to me. Keep me from being vain.

If I am smart and do well in school, keep me from being puffed up or feeling that I am better than others whose brains work more slowly than mine. Teach me to always be aware of how small I am in this great world of yours, and how little cause I have to be conceited. In Jesus Christ's name, amen.

*James 1:17

WHEN I'M JEALOUS

Lord, You have given me my own special personality and all my gifts and talents. Forgive me for being jealous of those who seem to be prettier, or smarter, or richer, or more popular than I am. Teach me to work for those things I envy in them. Make me able to praise what I admire in them. Keep me from trying to tear them down by making fun or talking behind their backs. Clean my heart of jealousy, because it will only bring me unhappiness. In Jesus' name, amen.

WHEN I'M SAD

Lord, my sorrow is too much for me, and I can't escape from it. Take my burdens. In Your life on earth You were a "man of sorrows." You know what it is like to be sad. You know how hard this is. Feel sorry for me, for I am so little and weak. Keep me from being crushed by this load. Your love can support me now and bring me peace in the middle of my sadness. Teach me to trust in You like a refuge from a storm. In Your name, amen.

WHEN I'M HAPPY

God, You have filled my heart to overflowing with happiness today. Remind me to take it as coming from You. You have filled all Your creatures with the joy of life, so that we can be glad together when we are blessed. Teach me not to be selfish when I have something to be happy about, but to share it with those who are sad or discouraged. Teach me how to enjoy being happy to the fullest, so I will have many good memories to last all my life. I won't always be happy every day. Help me remember that today is a special gift and to take thankfully all the pleasure that is in it. In Jesus' name, amen.

PART III

Thank You, God

Oh, give thanks to the LORD, for He is good!
For His mercy endures forever.

PSALM 107:1

THANKS FOR
ANSWERED PRAYER

Lord, thank You for all Your many gifts. All good things come from You, and You have filled my life with blessings. You have given me food and clothes, a home and friends. You have given me useful chores to do and wholesome fun.

And now You have given me this special answer to prayer, satisfying the desire of my heart. What can I give back to You for all Your blessings? I can only give myself, asking You to help me enjoy my new gift in the right way. Teach me not to be selfish and to pray for others, too. Show me how to share the good things which You have given me. In Jesus' name, amen.

THANKS FOR LIFE

God, thank You for Your gift of life. You have given me a body made just right for my needs, and a mind to learn the wonders of Your world. You have made everything for me to enjoy. Help me to remember daily that I owe my life to You, and that I live in Your sight. Help me to do my best to please You while I am quick and strong. Keep me from being idle and getting into trouble. Help me to remember You, my Creator, now while I am young. In Jesus' name, amen.

THANKS FOR HOME

Heavenly Father, I praise You for giving me a good home. When I was a helpless baby my parents cared for me. Because they loved me they gave me everything I needed. Help me to remember how they have worked for me. When I am tempted to be impatient with their rules and restrictions, help me to remember Jesus, who loved and obeyed His parents. Keep me from sulking or being ungrateful. Show me how I can help make my home a happy place, for my family and everyone who comes to visit. In Your name, amen.

Bless, O Father, thy gifts to our use and us
to thy service. For Christ's sake, amen.

BOOK OF COMMON PRAYER

Be present at our table, Lord;
Be here and everywhere adored.
Thy creatures bless, and grant that we
May feast in paradise with Thee. Amen.

JOHN WESLEY

Come, Lord Jesus, be Thou our guest;
And let these gifts to us be blessed. Amen.

Lord God, heavenly Father, bless us and these thy gifts which we receive from thy bountiful goodness. Through Jesus Christ our Lord, amen.

Bless us, O Lord, in what we are about to receive, and make us truly thankful. For Jesus Christ's sake. Amen.

Give us grateful hearts, our Father, for all thy mercies, and make us mindful of the needs of others. Through Jesus Christ our Lord, amen.

BOOK OF COMMON PRAYER

Great God, Thou Giver of all good,
Accept our praise, and bless our food,
Grace, health, and strength to us afford,
Through Jesus Christ, our blessed Lord.
                                    Amen.

Thou openest Thy hand, O Lord,
The earth is filled with good;
Teach us with thankful hearts to take
From Thee our daily food. Amen.

Thou hast given so much to me,
Give one thing more—a grateful heart;
Not thankful when it pleaseth me,
As if Thy blessings had spare days,
But such a heart whose pulse may be
Thy praise.

GEORGE HERBERT

Father, we thank Thee for the night
And for the pleasant morning light
For rest and food and loving care,
And all that makes the day so fair.

Help us to do the things we should
To be to others kind and good,
In all we do, in all we say,
To grow more loving every day. Amen.

For the night's rest, the morning meal, the new day and all the blessings it may bring, we give Thee grateful thanks, our Father. Help us to serve Thee by serving our fellowman. Through Jesus Christ our Lord, amen.

PART IV

Special Times

Rejoice always; pray without ceasing; in everything give thanks; for this is the will of God in Christ Jesus for you.

1 THESSALONIANS 5:16–18

IN THE MORNING

Thank You, God, for keeping me safe through the night. Be with me today and make me aware of Your Holy Spirit. Guide me in everything I do and say. Keep my tongue from unkind and careless words, and keep my mind pure. Make me diligent in my activities, cheerful, and thoughtful of others. Rescue me when I am in danger of giving in to temptation. Help me to make right decisions. In Jesus' name, amen.

AT NOON

Lord, keep me from getting too busy to think about You. In Jesus' name, amen.

AT BEDTIME

Praise You, God, for Your love and mercy. Thank You for being with me today. Forgive me for the things I have done wrong, and help me to do better tomorrow. Make me grateful for the people who have been kind to me, and help me to forgive those who have hurt me. Give me a restful night so that I will be ready for tomorrow, both in mind and body. Strengthen and refresh me with sleep. Bless my loved ones and me. In Jesus' name, amen.

ON MY BIRTHDAY

Lord, You have given me another year of life. Teach me how to live each year as one of Your children. Your almighty protection is all around me, and I am sheltered by Your love. Keep me from evil.

Turn my thoughts to what is good, so that I will serve You with a willing mind. Help me not to forget how short and unpredictable my life is. Make me live each day so that You will be pleased with me. Give me deep thankfulness for Your love, the love of my parents, and for my many blessings. In Jesus' name, amen.

ON VACATION

God, please protect me on this trip and keep me in Your loving care. Make me quick to see the beauty in Your world and to appreciate it. Help me not to miss anything interesting or fun, so I will have lots of good things to remember when I get back home. There are so many things to think about, but I don't want to forget You. Show me how perfect Your handiwork is, so I can praise You better. In Jesus' name, amen.

ON A TRIP

Lord, I have traveled far today, but I have not left You behind. Many miles separate me from my home and friends, but not from You. You are with me always. I praise You for Your care. Watch over me and keep me safe while I'm traveling. Open my eyes to see the beauty of Your world and the wonderful work of Your hands. Bless my family while I'm away. In Jesus' name, amen.

ON A VISIT

Heavenly Father, You have given me good friends. Watch over them and me while I visit with them. Help me to remember that I am their guest and many things are being done for my pleasure.

Remind me at all times to be grateful. Help me to show my thanks by seeing ways to help. Make me think of ways to make this visit a blessing to my friend and to myself. Remember the many boys and girls who are not so fortunate, and bring them friends who will be good to them. In Jesus' name, amen.

AT CAMP

Lord Jesus, be with us and bless our camp. You took Your disciples into the mountains by themselves with no tent but the sky. You ate with them by the sea. With You they lived in the open and learned the ways of God in nature. You taught them on the hillside and walked with them through the fields.

Walk with us and talk with us in the days we spend together here. I want our camp life to be filled with Your companionship. Teach us here how to be free from worry and how to trust in You for everything we need. Keep us safe in all our outdoor sports. Thank You for those who made this camp possible. In Your name, amen.

ON A HIKE

Lord Jesus Christ, You often walked with Your disciples through the fields and by the sea. You pointed out to them the birds and the flowers, the sky and the trees. You slept under the stars and ate out in the fields.

Be with us today. Help us to see the beautiful things on earth and in the sky that are signs of our heavenly Father's love. When we are tired and hungry, make us think of how You had nowhere to lay Your head, and how You picked grain for food. Teach us to thank You joyfully for the world around us. Watch over us and bring us safely home. In Your name, amen.

WHEN MY PARENTS ARE AWAY

Heavenly Father, please bless and keep my parents while they are far away. Watch over them and me while we are separated. Keep them from sickness and protect them from all danger. Keep me from being lonely or afraid. Make me faithful in the things I should do. Help me to make their return happy by doing my work and bringing honor to our family name. In Jesus' name, amen.

WHEN A FRIEND DIES

Lord Jesus, You cried when Your friend Lazarus died. You know how I feel, too. Please comfort me. Help me to realize that life on earth is the beginning, not the end. Your love and mercy surround Your children here, and You go with us through death to eternal life. Thank You that if my friend knew You, she has gone to be with You, amen.

BEFORE THE GAME

God, Your Word teaches me to tell You all my requests in prayer. So I'm asking You to go with me in this game. Put my mind in order so that I will have my body under control. Keep my heart so that I will not lose my temper. Make me calm when the pressure is on. When I am provoked, give me self-control. Help me to remember that he who controls his temper is better than he who conquers the city.* Keep me within the rules of the game, and help me be honest and fair in play. For Your name's sake, amen.

---

*Proverbs 16:32

WHEN I WIN

Lord, thank You that You are with me when I win. Thank You for controlling my temper and helping me play fair. I praise You for my success. Keep me now from boasting and being overconfident the next time I play. May I remember that pride goes before destruction and a haughty spirit before a fall.* Teach me to trust in You for victory. For Your name's sake, amen.

---

*Proverbs 16:18

WHEN I LOSE

God, You comfort everyone who puts her trust in You. You know how hard it is to face failure. Help me not to be overwhelmed by my defeat. If it was my fault, help me to see my weaknesses and to do better next time. God, You can turn failure into success. Help me to learn how failure can be a blessing if it leads me to trust in You. Help me to learn that lesson now, and give me strength to try again. In Jesus' name, amen.

WHEN I'M IN PAIN

Dear Lord, it hurts so bad I can't think of anything but the pain. Help me to bear it. Make me remember how You suffered here and how patient You were. Strengthen me so I can endure like a good soldier of Yours. Heal my body, so that the pain will go away. Bless the medicine that I am taking, so it will work. Keep me from complaining all the time, from being impatient, and from just giving up. When I feel better, remind me of how good You are and how You answered my prayers. I ask these things for Your sake, amen.

WHEN I'M SICK

Lord Jesus, when You were on earth You healed the sick. I'm asking You for help now because I am sick. Please be with me tonight. Time seems to pass very slowly when I don't feel well. But to You the night is as clear as the day. Comfort me when I am lonely, and reassure me when I am afraid. I know You are taking care of me, and soon You will make me well, amen.

IN THE HOSPITAL

Lord Jesus, please be with me now before they operate on me. You suffered for me on the Cross, and You know what it is like to be afraid. Help me to be brave now, and to trust You. Give the doctor skill and wisdom. Thank You that I will be asleep while he works and won't feel any pain. Please make me well, but also teach me how I can be a comfort to others right now. In Your dear name, amen.

WHEN I'M
GETTING WELL

Lord, thank You that I am feeling better. I pray now that I won't forget how You've helped me when I needed You so. I want to get well quickly. Keep me from being impatient and demanding. Help me not to talk about how sick I was or how awful I felt, but to think of others. Make me considerate of my mother and father and everyone who has taken care of me for so long. Help me to be cheerful and ready to do my chores and school work again with a willing mind. In Jesus' name, amen.

ON SUNDAY

God, You gave me this day of rest. Help me not to spend it on myself, but to make it Your day. First, I want to show that I believe in You by giving You praise and thanksgiving together with others who love You. Then, let me take the rest of the day and use it for what You made it: to rest my body and to refresh my soul. Make me free to feel the innocent pleasures that take me out into Your world of fresh air and sunshine. In Jesus' name, amen.

ON THANKSGIVING

God, You have given me and my family so many good things. Give us thankful hearts to enjoy everything from You. Make us grateful for the little things. Help us not to take anything for granted, but to realize they all are gifts from You. Thank You for the love in my family and for my comfortable home. If something is wrong and it is hard to give thanks now, make us feel how much You love us. Teach us how to trust in You perfectly. In Jesus' name, amen.

ON CHRISTMAS

Lord Jesus Christ, on this day You were born on earth a little child. Help me to keep in mind Your great gift and Your perfect life. May Your unselfish love make me thoughtful of others during this happy time. Open my eyes to see that giving and not getting is the lesson of this day. Fill my heart with praise for everything You have done for me and given me. Make me grateful for how kind and generous my friends are. Make me able to love everyone as You love me. In Your name, amen.

ON NEW YEAR'S DAY

God, You have given me a brand new year. Guide me and protect me all the months to come. You know everything I will say and do and where I will go. Brighten every good thing that happens with the sunshine of Your love. Give me Your strong support when I am in danger of doing wrong, and forgive me when I sin. In Jesus' name, amen.

ON EASTER

Lord of Glory, You broke the chains of death and rose from the grave to bring me a new life. Thank You for dying for me. You chose a woman to be the first witness of Your resurrection and to tell the good news to Your friends. Make me always ready to tell how You love me and how You are teaching me Your truth. Because You died and rose again, help me not to be afraid of death. Amen.

PART V

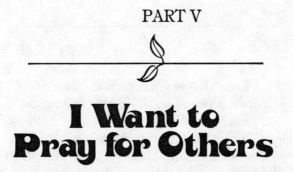

I Want to Pray for Others

I exhort first of all that supplications,
prayers, intercessions, and giving of thanks be made
for all men.

1 TIMOTHY 2:1

FOR MY CHURCH

Lord Jesus Christ, You have called everyone to confess You. Thank You for calling me. Thank You for putting into my heart the desire to be Your disciple. Thank You for my church, where I first confessed You as my Lord. Help me to be faithful to Your body of believers, and to love them as my spiritual family. In Jesus' name, amen.

FOR MY PASTOR

Lord, thank You for all the friends and teachers that help me to do right. I especially thank You for my pastor. Through his sympathy and interest I have learned to think more constantly of You. Bless him and keep him from all harm, and give him all the strength he needs for his work. Teach me how to listen better to Your Word as he teaches it. Show me how I can help him win other girls to You. In Your name, amen.

FOR PEOPLE WHO
ARE LONELY

Lord, You love each one of us equally. Look in tender mercy on people who feel neglected today. With You as their Friend, they will not feel alone. Make me more thoughtful of others and show me how I can bring comfort to those who are lonely. Keep me from getting too busy to notice who is lonely or sad. Teach me to be a good Samaritan and follow my love with service. In Jesus' name, amen.

FOR PEOPLE WHO
ARE NEEDY

God, Your name is Love. Hear my prayer for Your children who do not have enough to eat or wear. You have given me many good things. Open my eyes today to someone who is poor and hungry. Show me how I might help them. Show me how I can find friends for them. Lead me to other people who can help, too. Remind me how Jesus had no place to lay His head and how He was often without food. He called the poor His brothers, and blessed those who gave to them. In His name I pray, amen.

FOR PARENTS WHO
HAVE LOST A CHILD

Heavenly Father, thank You for my life. You have taken my friend, whose parents loved her as my parents love me. Comfort me. Comfort them, I ask, as only You can comfort. Help them to keep their eyes on You. Remind them that You are not far away. Speak to them in their sorrow as You are speaking to me. Help them to say, "Your will be done." Show me how I can comfort them. In Jesus' name, amen.

FOR A FRIEND
WHOSE PARENT
HAS DIED

Heavenly Father, thank You for my home. Help me to remember that I did not make it, but it is Your gift to me. Give me a thankful heart for my mother and father. Remember my friend whose parent has died. Be very near to her and more to her than a father or a mother. Give me the strength to stay with her, and show me how I can comfort her. Help us both to think of how wonderful heaven will be one day, when we are together with all those we love. In Jesus' name, amen.

FOR FRIENDS AND NEIGHBORS

God, bless my friends and neighbors. Watch over their homes and shield them from all evil. Protect their houses from fire, from thieves, and anything else that might destroy or bring them trouble. Help me to be thoughtful of their property. Show me how I can serve them. Make me a ready and willing friend and good neighbor. In Jesus' name, amen.

FOR THE WORLD

Lord, You are God over this world, for You have made us all. I want Your kingdom to come in all lands. I want Your will to be done by all people. I want the light of Your gospel to shine in all the dark places of this earth. I wish people everywhere would treat each other as brother and sister. Bless those missionaries who have gone to foreign countries and keep them safe. Guide my country to send only what is good to other countries and to keep from them whatever would harm or destroy. Defeat the wicked plans that lead to war; make the peace of Christ rule the world. For His name's sake, amen.

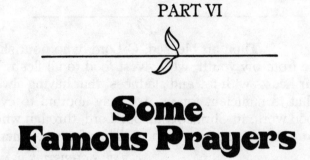

PART VI

Some
Famous Prayers

Thou art blessed, O Lord, who nourishest me from my youth, who givest food to all flesh. Fill our hearts with joy and gladness, that having always what is sufficient for us, we may abound to every good work, in Christ Jesus our Lord, through whom glory, honor, and power be to Thee forever, amen.

EARLY CHRISTIAN PRAYER

Give perfection to beginners, O Father. Give intelligence to the little ones; give aid to those who are running their course. Give sorrow to the negligent; give fervor of spirit to the lukewarm. Give to the perfect a good consummation. For the sake of Christ Jesus our Lord, amen.

IRENEUS

Look upon us, O Lord, and let all the darkness of our souls vanish before the beams of Thy brightness. Fill us with holy love, and open to us the treasures of Thy wisdom. All our desire is known to Thee. Therefore perfect what Thou hast begun and what Thy Spirit hast awakened us to ask in prayer. We seek Thy face; turn Thy face unto us and show us Thy glory. Then shall our longing be satisfied and our peace shall be perfect. Through Jesus Christ our Lord, amen.

ST. AUGUSTINE

Thanks be to Thee, my Lord Jesus Christ,
For all the benefits which Thou hast given me,
For all the pains and insults which Thou hast
  borne for me,
O most merciful Redeemer, Friend, and Brother.
May I know Thee more clearly,
Love Thee more dearly,
And follow Thee more nearly
Day by day.

ST. RICHARD

Teach us, good Lord, to serve Thee as Thou deservest; to give and not to count the cost; to fight and not to heed the wounds; to toil and not to seek for rest; to labor and not to ask for any reward, save that of knowing that we do Thy will. Through Jesus Christ our Lord, amen.

IGNATIUS LOYOLA

Praise ye and bless the Lord, and give thanks unto Him, and serve Him with great humility. Amen.

ST. FRANCIS OF ASSISI

Lord, make me the instrument of Thy peace. Where there is hatred, let me sow love; where there is injury, pardon; where there is doubt, faith; where there is despair, hope; where there is darkness, light; and where there is sadness, joy.

O Divine Master, grant that I may not so much seek to be consoled as to console; to be understood as to understand; to be loved as to love: for it is in giving that we receive, it is in pardoning that we are pardoned, and it is in dying that we are born to eternal life. Amen.

ST. FRANCIS OF ASSISI

May the strength of God pilot us.
May the power of God preserve us.
May the wisdom of God instruct us.
May the hand of God protect us.
May the way of God direct us.
May the shield of God defend us.
May the host of God guard us against the
   snares of the Evil One and the temptations
   of the world.
May Christ be with us.
Christ before us.
Christ over us.
May thy salvation, O Lord, be always ours this day
And forevermore, amen.

ST. PATRICK

In confidence of Thy goodness and great mercy, O Lord, I draw near unto Thee, as a sick person to the Healer, as one hungry and thirsty to the Fountain of life, a creature to the Creator, a desolate soul to my own tender Comforter. Behold, in Thee is all whatsoever I can or ought to desire; Thou art my Salvation and my Redemption, my Hope and my Strength. Rejoice therefore this day the soul of Thy servant; for unto Thee, O Lord, have I lifted up my soul. Amen.

THOMAS À KEMPIS

O Lord, let us not live to be useless. Amen.

JOHN WESLEY

My Own
Special Prayers

As I lay me down to sleep,
I pray the lord my soul to keep,
And if I shall die before I wake I pray the lord my soul to take.

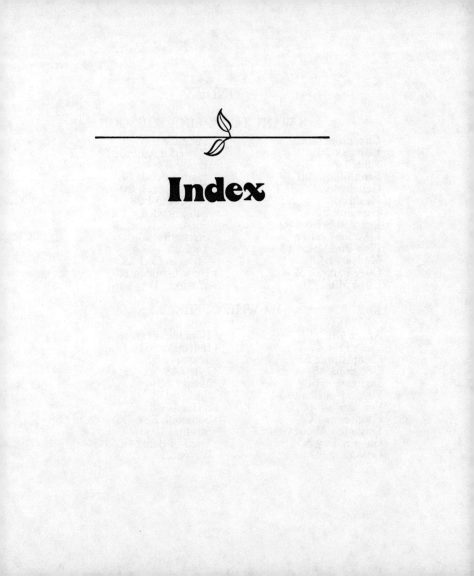

Index

INDEX

I. I WANT TO BE LIKE YOU, GOD

II. WHEN I FEEL . . .

III. THANK YOU, GOD

IV. SPECIAL TIMES

V. I WANT TO PRAY FOR OTHERS

VI. SOME FAMOUS PRAYERS

MY OWN SPECIAL PRAYERS 121